Classic Easy Dip Recipes

Dive into These Quick and Easy Dip Recipes That Will Have You Rethinking Your Cheese Board!

BY

Daniel Humphreys

Copyright 2019 Daniel Humphreys

License Notes

No part of this Book can be reproduced in any form or by any means including print, electronic, scanning or photocopying unless prior permission is granted by the author.

All ideas, suggestions and guidelines mentioned here are written for informative purposes. While the author has taken every possible step to ensure accuracy, all readers are advised to follow information at their own risk. The author cannot be held responsible for personal and/or commercial damages in case of misinterpreting and misunderstanding any part of this Book

Table of Contents

Introduction 6

    Tszaski 8

    Creamy chickpea 10

    Roast Pumpkin 12

    Ricotta lemon 15

    Roast tomato basil 17

    Classic pesto 20

    Chunky Cashew 22

    Roast Eggplant 24

    Cream cheese sesame 26

    Middle Eastern 28

    Smoked Paprika 31

    Guacamole 33

Sweet Chili Avocado 35

Lentil Tomato.. 37

Tomato olive 39

Creamy Pea 41

Roast Capsicum 43

Feta Spinach 45

Mediterranean tuna 47

Toasted Pumpkin Seed.. 49

Roast Almond 51

Mexican tomato 54

Sundried tomato 57

Garden herbs 59

Sweet beetroot... 61

Cannellini chili.. 64

Asian dipping sauce 66

Sweet Carrot.. 68

Swiss Gruyere cheese melt 71

Lentil Avocado.. 73

Conclusion 75

Author's Afterthoughts.. 76

About the Author 77

Introduction

Time definitely isn't a luxury if you have kids, work 9 to 5 or are overwhelmed with household chores. That's why we've created this recipe book filled with easy and delicious dip recipes that will become your new best friend at snack time.

Whether it's between end of school and dinner or to pair with crackers on a cheeseboard, there is a dip recipe for everyone, and we know you'll find your new favorite one inside this book.

From the classic greek style tzatziki to the more modern roast pumpkin, this recipe book will open your eyes to the world of dippable ingredients and have you opening your mind to trying new ingredients you wouldn't immediately think to use.

The dip game has changed, there's no room for store-bought pesto and hummus once you try these brilliant and delicious recipes out. So what are you waiting for? Dip in!

Tszaski

This classic dip will take you on a trip to Greece with its creamy, herby freshness. Enjoy this tszaski the traditional way spread over freshly cooked flatbread or toasted french stick. This dip is also the perfect side dish for any greek or indian style meal.

Ingredients:

- 1 cup plain Greek yogurt
- ¼ cup cucumber (diced finely)
- Juice of 1 lemon
- 1 clove garlic
- Small bunch fresh coriander

Instructions:

1. Finely dice the cucumber, garlic, and coriander, then place all into a small serving bowl.

2. Add the yogurt and lemon juice then mix together well with a fork.

3. Garnish with some more fresh coriander and enjoy spread on plain crackers or naan bread!

Creamy chickpea

You can't go wrong with this classic chickpea dip. With all the goodness of a homemade hummus and the slight flavor hit of cumin, this dip can be paired with all flavors on a cheeseboard or platter. Dip carrots, celery, crackers or cheese sticks into this classic.

Ingredients

- 1 can chickpeas, drained
- 4 Tbs extra virgin olive oil
- ¼ tsp sea salt
- ¼ tsp pepper
- Juice of ½ a lemon
- 4 Tbs tahini paste

Instructions

1. Place all Ingredients into a food processor or blender.

2. Pulse the mixture until you produce a smooth consistency (the odd chunky bit is good for texture)

3. Serve in a small bowl, and drizzle some more extra virgin olive oil on top a sprinkle of cumin seeds

Roast Pumpkin

This dip recipe turns pumpkin soup into the ultimate afternoon or before dinner snack. Perfect enjoyed on its own or with plain crackers, this roast pumpkin dip is the perfect winter dip to enjoy if you're needing something sweeter and delicious before a main meal.

Ingredients

- 1 can chickpeas, drained
- 4 Tbs extra virgin olive oil
- ¼ tsp sea salt
- ¼ tsp pepper
- Juice of ½ a lemon
- 4 Tbs tahini paste
- 1 cup pumpkin, cut into small cubes

Instructions

1. Preheat the oven to 190°C and line a baking tray with baking paper.

2. Chop the pumpkin up into small sized cubes and place onto the baking tray with a drizzle of olive over the top.

3. Place the pumpkin into the oven for 25 minutes or until golden orange.

4. Once the pumpkin is cooked, remove from the oven and let to cool down to room temperature.

5. Once the pumpkin is cool, place it with all of the other Ingredients into a food processor or blender.

6. Pulse the mixture until you produce a smooth consistency (the odd chunky bit is good for texture)

7. Serve in a small bowl, and drizzle some more extra virgin olive oil on top a sprinkle of cumin seeds

Ricotta lemon

With flavors of citrus, cream and cheese, this ricotta and lemon based dip is simply perfect for spreading on toast for lunch with fresh slices of avocado and a drizzle of olive oil. You can dress this dip up to suit any Italian or Greek style dish by garnishing with a dash of extra virgin olive oil or some freshly picked coriander.

Ingredients

- 250g smooth or spreadable ricotta
- Zest of 1 lemon
- Juice of ½ a lemon
- ¼ cup grated parmesan cheese
- ¼ tsp ground nutmeg

Instructions

1. Place all of the Ingredients into a small serving dish or bowl and mix well with a fork to combine.

2. You should produce a smooth, spreadable consistency with a cheesy flavor, with a slight lemon zing!

Roast tomato basil

This italian inspired dip will have everyone dipping in for seconds and thirds with its likeness to the classic spaghetti bolognese dish. This take on an italian classic is the perfect appetizer for an Italian style meal, introducing the taste buds to the hearty flavors of tomato, parmesan and basil.

Ingredients

- 1 punnet of cherry tomatoes
- 3 Tbs extra virgin olive oil
- ¼ cup grated parmesan cheese
- 10 basil leaves

Instructions

1. Preheat the oven to 180°C and line a baking tray with baking paper.

2. Place the cherry tomatoes, whole, onto the baking tray and bake in the preheated oven for 25 minutes, or until soft and slightly charred on the skin.

3. Remove the tomatoes from the oven and leave to cool for 20 minutes.

4. Once the tomatoes have cooled down, place them into a medium serving bowl and roughly mash up with a fork, producing a chunky texture.

5. Finely chop the basil leaves up

6. Place the olive oil grated parmesan cheese and basil into the tomatoes and mix with a fork to combine.

7. Serve with toasted crostini bread or ciabatta

Classic pesto

You can't go wrong with a classic pesto, and this recipe will make things a whole lot easier when it comes to making your own from scratch. Substitute the cashews and pine nuts out for any nut of your choice, or use sesame seeds if you are serving anyone with a nut allergy.

Ingredients

- ½ cup cashew nuts
- 2 Tbs pine nuts
- 15 basil leaves
- 5 Tbs extra virgin olive oil
- Squeeze of lemon juice

Instructions

1. Place all Ingredients into a blender or food processor and pulse to produce a coarse, semi-spreadable pesto

2. Serve with crackers and cheese on a cheeseboard.

Chunky Cashew

This is a twist on the classic chickpea dip or hummus, however with a great family hit of nutty flavor and goodness! You'll get your healthy fat intake in for the day with the good fats from the cashew nut.

Ingredients

- ½ cup cashew nuts
- ½ can chickpeas, drained
- 2 Tbs tahini paste
- 3 Tbs extra virgin olive oil
- ½ tsp ground cumin
- ¼ tsp ground sweet paprika

Instructions

1. Place all Ingredients into a food processor and pulse to combine and produce a smooth consistency, almost like nut butter

2. Serve spread on ciabatta or with crackers and carrot sticks to dip into

Roast Eggplant

You will soon be turning the heads of those who aren't fond of eggplant when you whip up this delicious eggplant dip. The smoky, charred flavors give this dip a truly comforting and delicious flavor like no other vegetable. Try dipping warm flatbread into this one for a true Greek style feast.

Ingredients

- 1 eggplant
- 3 Tbs extra virgin olive oil
- ½ tsp smoked paprika
- ¼ tsp ground cumin

Instructions

1. Preheat the oven to 180°C and line a baking tray with baking paper.

2. Cut up the eggplant into medium sized cubes and place onto the baking tray and bake in the preheated oven for 25 minutes, or until soft and slightly charred on the skin.

3. Remove the eggplant from the oven and leave to cool for 20 minutes.

4. Once the eggplant has cooled down, place them into a medium serving bowl and roughly mash up with a fork, producing a chunky texture.

5. Place the olive oil, cumin, and paprika into the eggplant and mix with a fork to combine.

6. Serve with toasted crostini bread or ciabatta

Cream cheese sesame

The ease of this dip will have you whipping it up every weekend for entertaining your family and guests. Try moulding the dip into a ball as best you can and rolling in grated cheese and sesame seeds to create a cheese ball! Everyone can dip their crackers into the ball for a fun and different pre-dinner snack.

Ingredients

- 250g cream cheese
- 4 Tbs tahini paste
- ¼ cup grated parmesan cheese
- ¼ cup grated tasty cheese
- 5 grinds of black pepper
- Small bunch fresh chives
- 1 Tbs sesame seeds

Instructions

1. Finely chop up the chives, and grate both the cheeses and set both aside

2. Place all of the Ingredients, including the cheeses and chives into a medium serving dish and mix well with a fork to completely combine.

3. You should produce a smooth, spreadable consistency

4. Garnish with more sesame seeds on top

Middle Eastern

The flavors of the middle east come together with this dip recipe, and whether you are a spice lover or not, this is a difficult one not to love! Try dipping naan bread or poppadoms into this dip to make it fun and more kid friendly.

Ingredients

- 1 eggplant
- ½ punnet cherry tomatoes
- 3 Tbs extra virgin olive oil
- ½ tsp smoked paprika
- ¼ tsp ground cumin
- ¼ tsp garam masala
- ¼ tsp ground coriander
- ¼ tsp ground cardamom

Instructions

1. Preheat the oven to 180°C and line a baking tray with baking paper.

2. Cut up the eggplant into medium sized cubes and place onto the baking with the whole cherry tomatoes tray and bake in the preheated oven for 25 minutes, or until soft and slightly charred on the skin.

3. Remove the eggplant and tomatoes from the oven and leave to cool for 20 minutes.

4. Once the eggplant and tomatoes have cooled down, place them into a medium serving bowl and roughly mash up with a fork, producing a chunky texture.

5. Place the olive oil and spices into the eggplant and mix with a fork to combine.

6. Serve with toasted crostini bread or ciabatta

Smoked Paprika

The creamy and smokiness of this smoked paprika dip turns the classic plain hummus into something special with a kick of smoky flavor. Perfect on a cheeseboard with plain crackers or even great spread on toast.

Ingredients

- 1 can chickpeas, drained
- 4 Tbs extra virgin olive oil
- ¼ tsp sea salt
- ¼ tsp pepper
- Juice of ½ a lemon
- 4 Tbs tahini paste
- 1 tsp smoked paprika

Instructions

1. Place all Ingredients into a food processor or blender.

2. Pulse the mixture until you produce a smooth consistency (the odd chunky bit is good for texture)

3. Serve in a small bowl, and drizzle some more extra virgin olive oil on top a sprinkle of smoked paprika

Guacamole

You really can't go wrong with a good guacamole. Perfect for serving with any Mexican style dish for some freshness, or even great spread on toast for a new twist on the classic avocado on toast.

Ingredients

- 2 avocados
- Juice and zest of 1 lemon
- ¼ cup smooth ricotta
- Salt and pepper to taste

Instructions

1. Place all Ingredients into a blender or food processor and pulse to combine, leaving the odd chunky piece of avocado to give texture to the dip.

2. Serve on fresh bread or as a side with a Mexican dish.

Sweet Chili Avocado

Almost like a guacamole, but not - this dip delivers the sweet and spicy flavor of the classic sweet chili sauce, with a relief of creamy avocado. This dip becomes the perfect appetizer for a Mexican style dish.

Ingredients

- 2 avocados
- Juice and zest of 1 lemon
- ¼ cup smooth ricotta
- Salt and pepper to taste

Instructions

1. Place all Ingredients into a blender or food processor and pulse to combine, leaving the odd chunky piece of avocado to give texture to the dip.

2. Serve on fresh bread or as a side with a Mexican dish.

Lentil Tomato

With the goodness of lentils and the high vitamin c content of tomatoes, this dip turns nutrition into a delicious afternoon treat. Try substituting the lentils in for chickpeas or cannellini beans for a different texture.

Ingredients

- ½ can lentils
- ¼ can crushed tomatoes
- 3 Tbs extra virgin olive oil
- Salt and pepper to taste

Instructions

1. Place all Ingredients into a small serving bowl and combine lightly with a spoon

2. Serve on fresh bread or toast or as a side to a middle eastern style dish

Tomato olive

This dip is the perfect one to serve on a hot summers afternoon with fresh bread and crackers. The freshness of the raw tomato and olives gives a relief from the hot sun, and is perfect served fridge cold.

Ingredients

- ⅓ cup kalamata olives, quartered
- 1 can crushed tomatoes
- 3 Tbs extra virgin olive oil
- Salt and pepper to taste

Instructions

1. Cut the olives up into quarters and place into a small serving bowl.

2. Place the rest of the Ingredients into the serving bowl with the olives and combine lightly with a spoon

3. Serve on fresh bread or toast or as a side to an italian style dish

Creamy Pea

This extra creamy pea dip is the perfect option for serving vegetables to your kids in disguise! This recipe is perfect when doubled and served as a side dish with schnitzel as a fresh alternative to the classic schnitzel, mashed potato and peas!

Ingredients

- 2 cups frozen peas
- ¼ cup cream
- 2 tbs butter
- Salt pepper to taste

Instructions

1. Place the peas in a small pot with hot water on the stove over a high heat. Boil for 6 minutes.

2. Drain the peas and transfer to a blender or food processor.

3. Place the cream, butter and salt and pepper into the blender and pulse to combine.

4. Blend the mixture until it is mostly smooth, however still with some chunky bits of peas.

Roast Capsicum

Ingredients

- 2 red capsicums
- 3 Tbs extra virgin olive oil
- ½ tsp smoked paprika
- ¼ tsp ground cumin

Instructions

1. Preheat the oven to 180°C and line a baking tray with baking paper.

2. Cut up the capsicums into slices and place onto the baking tray and bake in the preheated oven for 25 minutes, or until soft and slightly charred on the skin.

3. Remove the capsicum from the oven and leave to cool for 20 minutes.

4. Once the capsicum has cooled down, place them into blender or food processor.

5. Place the olive oil, cumin, and paprika into the blender as well and pulse to produce a smooth, slightly chunky texture.

6. Serve with toasted crostini bread or naan.

Feta Spinach

This pungent, yet garden fresh dip recipe is a great one to serve for a crowd of adults. This one is even great for piping into plain pastries or spread inside bread rolls for going on platters for a night of entertainment!

Ingredients

- 200g feta
- 1 cup fresh spinach
- 3 Tbs extra virgin olive oil
- Zest and juice of 1 lemon
- Small bunch of fresh coriander
- Salt pepper to taste

Instructions

1. Finely chop the spinach and coriander. Place into a small serving bowl

2. Place the rest of the Ingredients into the small serving bowl and mix well to combine.

3. Spread over crackers or toast with slices of avocado.

Mediterranean tuna

The kids will love this one just as much as the adults do! The ease of this one is true due to the fact everyone has extra cans of tuna somewhere in the back of their pantry. Try buying the canned tuna already flavored with tomato and basil for an extra hint of Italian flavor.

Ingredients

- 3 x 50g tins chunky tuna
- 5 basil leaves
- ¼ cup diced canned tomatoes
- ¼ cup parmesan cheese, grated
- Salt pepper to taste

Instructions

1. Roughly chop the basil and set aside.

2. Place all of the Ingredients, including the basil into a small serving bowl and mix well with a spoon to combine.

3. Perfect served with crackers or as a lunch box snack with bread.

Toasted Pumpkin Seed

This nutty twist on the classic hummus will become a popular one for the whole family. Try substituting pumpkin seeds for toasted sunflower or sesame seeds for a different kind of nutty flavor.

Ingredients

- 1 can chickpeas, drained
- 4 Tbs extra virgin olive oil
- ¼ tsp sea salt
- ¼ tsp pepper
- Juice of ½ a lemon
- 4 Tbs tahini paste
- ¼ cup pumpkin seeds

Instructions

1. Place the pumpkin seeds into a small frying pan and heat over a medium heat on the stove until they start to pop and puff up.

2. Set aside to cool for 10 minutes

3. Place all Ingredients, except the pumpkin seeds into a food processor or blender.

4. Pulse the mixture until you produce a smooth consistency (the odd chunky bit is good for texture)

5. Serve in a small bowl, and mix the pumpkin seeds through the dip to serve.

Roast Almond

This dip has a toasty flavor like none other, and takes the classic almond butter to a new, healthier level. Try using any nut of your choice for this recipe if you aren't a fan of almonds. Any nut will work just as perfectly!

Ingredients

- 1 can chickpeas, drained
- 4 Tbs extra virgin olive oil
- ¼ tsp sea salt
- ¼ tsp pepper
- Juice of ½ a lemon
- 4 Tbs tahini paste
- ¼ cup almonds

Instructions

1. Place the almonds into a small frying pan and heat over a medium heat on the stove until they start to puff up slightly and brown.

2. Remove from the stove and set aside to cool for 10 minutes

3. Place all Ingredients into a food processor or blender, including the almonds

4. Pulse the mixture until you produce a smooth consistency (the odd chunky bit of almond is good for texture)

5. Serve in a small bowl, and drizzle some more extra virgin olive oil on top a sprinkle of chopped up toasted almonds

Mexican tomato

This lighter version of a classic Mexican mince dish is the perfect option to make lots of to serve as a vegetarian Mexican dinner option. Try adding in fresh capsicum and chili for more of a flavor kick!

Ingredients

- 1 punnet of cherry tomatoes
- 3 Tbs extra virgin olive oil
- ½ tsp ground cumin
- ½ tsp smoked paprika
- ¼ tsp ground coriander
- ⅛ tsp ground nutmeg
- A small sprinkle of chili flakes

Instructions

1. Preheat the oven to 180°C and line a baking tray with baking paper.

2. Place the cherry tomatoes, whole, onto the baking tray and bake in the preheated oven for 25 minutes, or until soft and slightly charred on the skin.

3. Remove the tomatoes from the oven and leave to cool for 20 minutes.

4. Once the tomatoes have cooled down, place them into a medium serving bowl and roughly mash up with a fork, producing a chunky texture.

5. Place all of the spices and chili into a small frying pan and heat over a medium heat until fragrant.

6. Set aside to cool for 5 minutes then add to the tomatoes and mix thoroughly through.

7. Serve with nacho chips

Sundried tomato

This sweet sundried tomato dip is a stronger version of the tomato and basil dip, with a bolder, more concentrated flavor. This one is perfect for using as a salsa for Mexican food or for dipping sausages or other meat into instead of tomato sauce.

Ingredients

- ½ cup sun-dried tomatoes
- 3 Tbs extra virgin olive oil
- ¼ cup grated parmesan cheese
- 10 basil leaves

Instructions

1. Place all of the Ingredients into a food processor and pulse to combine until you produce a slightly chunky texture.

2. Serve on a cheese board with crackers and cheese.

Garden herbs

For a garden fresh and healthy option, this garden herb inspired dip is as good as it gets! Try using any herb of your choice from chives to mint or thyme - any flavor will work which makes this dip so unique in its flavor flexibility!

Ingredients

- 1 can chickpeas, drained
- 4 Tbs extra virgin olive oil
- ¼ tsp sea salt
- ¼ tsp pepper
- Juice of ½ a lemon
- 4 Tbs tahini paste
- Small bunch fresh coriander
- Small bunch fresh parsley

Instructions

1. Place all Ingredients into a food processor or blender.

2. Pulse the mixture until you produce a smooth consistency (the odd chunky bit is good for texture)

3. Serve in a small bowl, and drizzle some more extra virgin olive oil on top a sprinkle of chopped parsley or coriander

Sweet beetroot

This deliciously sweet and flavoursome beetroot dip is undoubtedly a true crowd pleaser on a cheeseboard. This one is also perfect put into the kids lunchboxes with some carrot and celery sticks for a sweet yet healthy morning tea option!

Ingredients

- 1 large beetroot
- 1 can chickpeas, drained
- 4 Tbs extra virgin olive oil
- ¼ tsp sea salt
- ¼ tsp pepper
- Juice of ½ a lemon
- 4 Tbs tahini paste

Instructions

1. Preheat the oven to 180°C and line a baking tray with baking paper

2. Cut the beetroot up into small cubes and place on the oven tray. Bake in the oven for 30 minutes or until soft and bright purple.

3. Remove the beetroot from the oven once cooked and set aside to cook for 20 minutes

4. Place all Ingredients into a food processor, including the beetroot.

5. Pulse the mixture until you produce a very smooth, consistency.

6. Serve in a small bowl, and drizzle some more extra virgin olive oil on top.

Cannellini chili

This lighter, less spicy take on a Mexican dish turns plain cannellini beans into something amazing with the subtle flavors of chini and paprika. Try adding in a squeeze of lemon or lime for a fresh hit on a hot day.

Ingredients

- 1 can white cannellini beans, drained
- ½ chili, diced finely
- 4 Tbs tahini paste
- Salt pepper to taste
- ½ tsp sweet paprika

Instructions

1. Place all Ingredients into a medium sized serving bowl and lightly crush the cannellini beans through the mixture with a fork.

2. You should pro

3. duce a chunky dip with pieces of beans and the smoothness of tahini.

Asian dipping sauce

This dipping sauce can be used for quite literally any Asian, Japanese or Chinese inspired dish. Whether it's used for dipping in dumplings, as a sauce for sushi or for flavoring a fried rice, this recipe ticks all of the boxes!

Ingredients

- ¼ soy sauce
- 1 Tbs hoisin sauce
- 1 Tsp sesame oil
- 3 Tbs mirin
- 2 Tbs grated fresh ginger
- ½ tsp brown sugar

Instructions

1. Grate the ginger into a small bowl.

2. Place all Ingredients into the small bowl with the ginger and mix with a spoon to combine or until the sugar is dissolved.

3. Perfect for dipping dumplings or spring rolls into.

Sweet Carrot

The great flavor and color of this sweet carrot dip will have the kids scoffing down hidden goodness even though they don't know it! You can use any vegetable from beetroot to sweet potato or swede as a substitute for carrot if you'd like to change the flavor up a bit.

Ingredients

- 3 medium carrots
- 1 can chickpeas, drained
- 4 Tbs extra virgin olive oil
- ¼ tsp sea salt
- ¼ tsp pepper
- Juice of ½ a lemon
- 4 Tbs tahini paste

Instructions

1. Preheat the oven to 180°C and line a baking tray with baking paper

2. Cut the carrot up into small rounds and place on the oven tray. Bake in the oven for 30 minutes or until soft and bright orange.

3. Remove the carrot from the oven once cooked and set aside to cook for 20 minutes

4. Place all Ingredients into a food processor, including the carrot.

5. Pulse the mixture until you produce a very smooth, consistency.

6. Serve in a small bowl, and drizzle some more extra virgin olive oil on top.

Swiss Gruyere cheese melt

This recipe is perfect to use as a fondue is you double the recipe. Serve it on top of a gas burner to stop the cheese from setting, and enjoy with friends for a fun fondue night!

Ingredients

- 100g Swiss cheese
- 100g Gruyere cheese
- ¼ cup white wine
- 1 clove garlic

Instructions

1. Place the garlic into a garlic crusher and crush into a small pot.

2. Place the pot over a low heat on the stove and cook until fragrant, but not browned.

3. Place the wine into the pot and bring to the boil

4. Grate both kinds of cheese into the pot and mix with a whisk constantly to combine and produce a smooth, semi-stringy mixture.

5. Serve immediately with chopped up vegetables to dip in.

Lentil Avocado

The goodness of fiber and vitamins is achieved inside this delicious dip. A take on the classic guacamole will give your kids their fiber intake for the day with the high fiber content of the lentils and healthy fat from the avocado.

Ingredients

- 2 avocados
- Juice and zest of 1 lemon
- ¼ cup smooth ricotta
- ½ can lentils, drained
- Salt and pepper to taste

Instructions

1. Place all Ingredients into a blender or food processor and pulse to combine, leaving the odd chunky piece of avocado to give texture to the dip.

2. Remove from the blender and mix the whole lentils through the avocado dip.

3. Serve on fresh bread or as a side with a Mexican dish.

Conclusion

So, there you have it! We have provided you with a bible of the best and most delicious dip recipes for any occasion. With the versatility of these recipes, and the ability to chop and change Ingredients to suit your liking and particular tastes makes this recipe book one of the best!

We hope you have discovered new flavors you never thought to try, especially in the form of a dip! Whether its entertaining for a big crowd, a family dinner or just a simple after school snack, this recipe book is filled with options for you to try and more importantly, please every taster!

So, what's the next step after you've mastered the art of dip making? Well now the world of dips is your oyster as this recipe book has surely taught you how to use sometimes unconventional and unfamiliar Ingredients and turn them into a tasty, nutritious treat.

So, what are you waiting for? Pick a new ingredient and turn it into a new and delicious dip!

Author's Afterthoughts

Thanks ever so much to each of my cherished readers for investing the time to read this book!

I know you could have picked from many other books but you chose this one. So a big thanks for downloading this book and reading all the way to the end.

If you enjoyed this book or received value from it, I'd like to ask you for a favor. Please take a few minutes to post an honest and heartfelt review on Amazon.com. Your support does make a difference and helps to benefit other people.

Thanks!

Daniel Humphreys

About the Author

Daniel Humphreys

Many people will ask me if I am German or Norman, and my answer is that I am 100% unique! Joking aside, I owe my cooking influence mainly to my mother who was British! I can certainly make a mean Sheppard's pie, but when it comes to preparing Bratwurst sausages and drinking beer with friends, I am also all in!

I am taking you on this culinary journey with me and hope you can appreciate my diversified background. In my 15 years career as a chef, I never had a dish returned to me by one of clients, so that should say something about me! Actually, I will take that back. My worst critic is my four years old son, who refuses to taste anything that is green color. That shall pass, I am sure.

My hope is to help my children discover the joy of cooking and sharing their creations with their loved ones, like I did all my life. When you develop a passion for cooking and my suspicious is that you have one as well, it usually sticks for life. The best advice I can give anyone as a professional chef is invest. Invest your time, your heart in each meal you are creating. Invest also a little money in good cooking hardware and quality ingredients. But most of all enjoy every meal you prepare with YOUR friends and family!

Made in United States
Troutdale, OR
04/12/2024

19149909R00051